third eye

an imprint of Skywriter Books

SKYWRITER BOOKS

iii
third eye

No portion of this book may be reproduced or transmitted in any form or by any means, electronic or mechanical, including photocopying, recording, or by an information storage and retrieval system—with the exception of a reviewer who may quote brief passages in a review to be printed in a newspaper or magazine—without written permission of the publisher. For information, contact Skywriter Books, PO Box 2630 Sausalito, CA 94966.

Published in the United States by Third Eye,
an imprint of Skywriter Books, Sausalito, California
www.skywriterbooks.com.

Skywriter Books, SkyMountain design and Third Eye
are registered trademarks of One Pink Hat Corp.

Skywriter Books is a member of IBPA,
Independent Book Publishing Association.

5 7 10 8 6

Copyright © Ushi Patel, 2013
All rights reserved

LIBRARY OF CONGRESS CATALOGUING-IN-PUBLICATION DATA

Patel, Ushi.
Brave the Unknown/ Ushi Patel.
p. cm.
ISBN 978-09822797-0-0
I. Title.
811'.269—P274   2013937044

Printed in the United States of America

Designed by Julie Munsyac

ATTN: Quantity Discounts Are Available to Your Company, Non-Profit, Educational Institution or Writing Organization for reselling, educational purposes, subscription incentives, gifts or fundraising campaigns.

For more information, please contact the publisher at
Skywriter Books, PO Box 2630, Sausalito, CA 94966
info@skywriterbooks.com.

WWW.SKYWRITERBOOKS.COM

BRAVE THE UNKNOWN

POEMS

USHI PATEL

SKYWRITER

FOR MY LINEAGE

CONTENTS

A Lion's Heart	11
Separation	13
A Poem for Timber	15
Born of Shadow	17
Red	19
Mistaken	21
Weighing the Heart	23
Freedom Fighter	25
Uninvited	27
Thorns	29
What Must Be Done	31
Luminous Night	33
A Crowded Street	35
Below the Ruins	37
The Vagrant's Boon	39
Worthy	41
The Promise of You	43
The Lovesmiths	45
Adagio	47
Africa	49
Dear	51
Luscious	53
Hum of the Heart	55
Make Your Mark	57
Infectious	59

The Death of The Punisher	61
Kindred	63
Blackborough Refuge	64
The Disturbed	67
Guardians of Humanity	69
Flawless	71
At Home in this Body	73
Unearthed	75
Temptress	77
Heartstrings	79
Fruition	81
The Wind's Reverie	83
Invincible	85
Throb	87
Surrender	89
When Horses Run	91
Victory	93
Pranks and Crimes	95
Midnight Blossom	97
A Poem's Mystery	99
Chased	101
Here	103
Savage Compassion	105
Seen	107

A LION'S HEART

Brave the unknown.
Trust the stirring in your heart
to voyage the fierce, uncharted territory
belonging solely to you.
Walk the path of the lionhearted
to the realm
where the darkness is pregnant.
Come to peace with the mischief before you,
the sun and the storm
will endow
a rainfall that ends
the famine of this era.

SEPARATION

Beloved,
you have become silent.
What is this strange land,
once fragrant with plenty,
now stark?
I search every suffocating corner,
in the caves I fear,
in the depths I have not yet traveled,
and in the places you played
your music,
the unlit roadsides you once roamed,
enchanter.
You run.
You stole my affection and much more,
master thief,
your ancient tricks are working,
in this vast nothingness,
I too, grow silent.

A POEM FOR TIMBER

You pranced
into the hollow of my heart
and hunted the emptiness,
chasing the lonely,
dampening me with your love.
You arrested my world
with your naughty and play.
And then, my loyal wolf friend,
in a merciless hack of our memoir
you are no longer mine, nor I yours.

Sweet Timber.
Where is the solace
at the end of these sobs,
why has life been cruel?

Then, from the recesses of grief,
a sweeping rumble,
an advancing wind,
your spirit ever in pursuit,
your paw prints
permanent
throughout my soul.

BORN OF SHADOW

The fraud
has pillaged this innocence,
and yet gone on to father an angel
in the arms of beauty and riches.
He came in the night
and took something
that I didn't even know I had.

Why then, God,
do you not take something
from that cheat,
so I may find whatever
peace I can
with a wretched crossing,
a silent, unaccounted abuse,
a burden that shadows me
wherever I go?

Was this the only way
a poet could be born?

RED

Lady accomplice,
you only snatched my pain
in your endeavor to steal love,
ridding me of the rogue within,
who has stripped rubies
from the walls of my heart
for far too long.

The man you think you have,
he tosses love,
as he often did cherry pits,
flung into the bay
after his tongue was pleasured.
As he will do with you,
slippery beauty,
whose mermaid tendrils
have briefly hooked his greed,
sinking both your minds in dark waters.

Ah,
this is the mend you too seek,
a marvelous betrayal
by the divine.

MISTAKEN

There is a certain tribe
who drags you
to the doorstep of the Beloved
with the idiotic way
they mistake you for a mule,
a conclusion they cleverly derived
from the constant droop
of your mouth and shoulders.
When you arrive
at that threshold of a master,
rip the ill-fitting saddle
from your back
and raise a flag in
the fortress of your soul.

WEIGHING THE HEART

Come death,
take this breath as your own,
return this body,
now disintegrating flesh and bone,
to hers,
keeper of the great remedy,
the empyrean Earth,
resplendent,
devouring,
complete.
She remembers me.
Awaiting, ever-ready
to affirm another resurrection.

Come death,
I have died a thousand times before.
I recognize
your sweltering glance,
vivid with terror,
here, as always,
early.

FREEDOM FIGHTER

A harrowing wind blows
with the memory of
weathered and wounded
sons and daughters,
broken,
embattled in another man's
futile struggle
for might,
a fabricated cause to
justify the blood.
Our freedom is not won
by the land we claim,
but by the mountains we climb,
in the lawless
countries of the heart.

UNINVITED

I let you enter uninvited,
prisoner of reality,
politician of limitation.
Hold your venomous tongue,
the smell of that stale breath
makes me ill.
I am not of this poor, lonely
tribe, I fly with the eagle.

Dreamers are awake.
Let them rest
in hope's arms
and drink her medicine.
Let them be ruined
by the sacred.

A queen beats
on your door,
but you refuse to let her in.

THORNS

What message
do you bring,
discomfort?
Though your entrance is
disturbing, often painful,
I know you are the bearer
of something vital
and wanted.

Let me sit with you
some moments more,
to penetrate the
meaning of your visit
and blaze a revolution
with the embers
of a ruthless fire
ravaging the brambles
that besiege my heart.

WHAT MUST BE DONE

Stagnation
finds a home
in the compound
where
anger resides,
built on a
foundation of
disappointment,
fortified by
walls of
resentment.
Strike a match,
ignite a fire,
turn this place to ash.
Let blame burn.

LUMINOUS NIGHT

Remember death
every day,
let go of
any idea of tomorrow,
what you think you must have,
and how life ought to be.
Time unfolds as it will.
Relinquish
any notion of fairness,
guarantee, and an easier way.
Unshackle the grip of possession,
shed your mask,
return.
Dusk draws the dawn near,
as all of nature knows,
die to live.

A CROWDED STREET

Heart,
I forgot you,
trying to survive life,
restless,
lost in the arrogance
of busy schemes,
enslaved by importance.
Then I saw you
on a crowded street
in the form of a dark,
radiant vagabond,
whose loving glance
flung open the cell doors,
cracking and crumbling
the hardened walls
this sad prisoner
had foolishly built.

BELOW THE RUINS

There is a
buried kingdom
in the loneliness
you run from,
the doubt that
governs most of
your choice.
Crawl into the cracks
of your hope
and indulge me in a dig.
Just beneath the
rubble of grief
is a haven of belief
where the Beloved barters
pearls and diamonds
in exchange for your tears.

THE VAGRANT'S BOON

I passed a homeless man today.
The odd, frightening fool,
remnants of a 16th century
religious cleric,
dirty,
hollow,
reeking sour.
He furiously
plucked garbage
from the street
around his roofless home.
As the shadow and light
pulsed in his cryptic eyes,
he lamented,
 "By whose authority
do you trash
this palace floor?"

WORTHY

"I am not enough,"
is the anthem of demons,
who are ruled by scarcity
and look in the glass of
everyone else's eyes
to know their significance.

Crush that mirror,
with the hammer of
kindness.

See yourself
in the sapphire shimmer
from the oceans within.

You are worthy
of all the riches
from love's spoils,
secured in the
unseen vault of the heart.

THE PROMISE OF YOU

Rise
like the sun.
Paint your hue across
the open sky.
Drench the trees
in the luster of your dreams,
they thirst for renewal.
Stroke the fields,
they wear morning's jewels
also yearning for your touch.
The water,
she too longs for your dancing feet,
scintillating,
enthralling,
softening the wanderer
weary from midnight's grip.

THE LOVESMITHS

Stroll alongside the
invisible giants, who
sweat and burn
for another's freedom.
Roam with the
cloaked heroes,
who endure
for love's uprising.
Wander the quiet alleys
where they weld together,
rebellious,
resolute,
hoping a spark
ignites an uncontrollable fire.

ADAGIO

Sit for a while,
descend.
Let the emptiness
undo you.
Let the burden
and worry
decay.
Submit to the calm.
Let the steady,
even sway
surround you.
Surrender
to the solitude.
Touch the
intimacy.
Become One.

AFRICA

Revere the ancient,
wrinkled elephant,
and her beautiful recognition of
tribal bones.

Marvel at the content,
surrendered river,
and her loving service to the sun.

Behold the benevolent,
regal mountain,
and her just offering of
protection.

Admire the boundless,
open sky
and her rendering of
many moods.

Reflect on the ancient,
ever-new moon,
and her steady witness
to earth's ebb and flow.

DEAR

May I
know the source
of the soft,
bewitching smile that
plays endlessly on
your perfect lips.

LUSCIOUS

The earth beckons
the rain upon her breast,
calling the sun to permeate
her womb and
the moon to ready her herbs.
She births,
a dazzling variety.
Look, there are figs,
succulent pomegranates,
the fleshy plums and peaches,
and so many more,
wanting to be savored,
longing for the touch of your lips,
hungry to play on your tongue,
and pour nectar
into the rivers of your body.

HUM OF THE HEART

Listen,
the drunken melody
of humming bees
beckons you
to the earthen tavern
where they serve
a lovely booze.

Sip the exquisite elixir
distilled from the notes
of their elated song.
Let it coat your throat,
gradually dripping down
the curves of your voice,
curing empty words
anxious to spill out raw.

Now,
I hear you.
Bright, resonant,
ripened by their sound.

MAKE YOUR MARK

Climb out
of despair
on a ladder
of the Beloved's tears.
Grace the pages
of time
with your triumph,
every letter
in your story is
an unopened gift,
dreaming of your
artistry,
crying for a freedom
only you can grant.

INFECTIOUS

Kindness kills
the sneaky
bitterness
that multiplies
in you
from decades of
putting yourself
last.

THE DEATH OF THE PUNISHER

When did I begin
calling upon you
as the great judge,
the One who burns the wicked?
When did I mistake you for
punisher,
shading the world in black and white?
The veil thins with
eyes of compassion
baring the absurdity
of deserving,
the sham of
shame, and
the countless,
concealed
births and deaths that
strangely
join this time to
this place.

KINDRED

Immigrant,

alone,

hopeful,

yours is a solemn journey,

as you navigate

an unknown fate,

by the light of

your lineage

and the promise

of freedom,

willing to let go,

trusting,

knowing what is dear

lives on within,

ready for any sacrifice

and the gifting of

generations

who can barely

pronounce your name.

BLACKBOROUGH REFUGE

In the black night,
trust the pierce of stars.
Those saintly bodies
will guide you through
the naked sea
of opinion and projection,
towards a misty, moonlit harbor.
Anchor there.
In the celebrated dawn,
persist by the streams of the sun,
those heavenly doorways
will true you across
the knotted valley
of compliment and praise,
towards the ageless,
mossy stronghold of humility.
Dwell there.

THE DISTURBED

As you move about
this mercurial realm,
many will
seduce time from your keep,
emptying your pockets,
stealing your merit,
unaware of
the blessed origin,
turning these riches into
mere coin
of survival and trade.

Where is your shield?
This fortune belongs
to the Bestower,
as does your life.
Remain devoted
to one.

GUARDIANS OF HUMANITY

Serve the forgotten.
The endangered
growing few,
natives of treetops
and understory.
Black-Crested Gibbons, Silky Shifakas,
and Three-Toed Sloths.
Caiques, Keas and Manakins.
The ring-tailed, bangled,
and spotted.
Orphans and migrants,
with tireless courage
and generosity
in the face of need.
They alone
protect humanity
from extinction,
one by one,
recovering
the fragments that remain.

FLAWLESS

Today someone searches
for a seer,
to look beyond mistakes,
a weaver of a different tale,
one who defies the villain within.

Go,
uncover the shamed,
tear the heavy, sullied garments
from their exhausted shoulders.
Lift them up.

AT HOME IN THIS BODY

Judgment dies
in the arms of
acceptance.
See what you wish
others would.
All your seeming
imperfections and
differences are
the Beloved's muse,
the lifeblood of
her infinite expression
pulsing through the
veins of billions.

UNEARTHED

Hey lonely,
I threw you out
with the cheating man
and his cowardly cohort,
then made love for hours
to the devil in the divine.
I woke, contented,
lit from within,
dripping with stars,
kissing the earth
and raining my
affection upon her.
She leaned in and smirked:
My dear,
I know
what you've been up to.

TEMPTRESS

I am a penniless beggar,
clenching my beat-up
cardboard sign
inked with the pledge,
"WILL WORK FOR LOVE."
I scout the street corners
where those singing heretics
have alleged
the Beloved deals,
desperate for her poison.

I willingly gave up my loot
for any whisper
of her whereabouts,
only to collide with even more
howling madmen
and addicted women.

Now, I bargain
these cherished lines.

I suspect,
by the increasing encounters
with her merciless hoodlums,
I finally have something
she wants.

HEARTSTRINGS

There is something
only you can offer,
tied to you
throughout time,
with the flowing,
honeyed
strands of the
creator's locks.
Come,
let's swing on them,
and weave
our thick, silky threads
through the beautiful,
frayed tapestry of life.

FRUITION

Command excellence
with your own
enthusiasm and
jubilant ways.
Fulfillment seeks a
garden,
fertile and wild,
teeming
with creepers and creatures,
tangles and thorns,
and many
buds and blooms,
all tended
by the steady hand
of a master.

THE WIND'S REVERIE

Breathe your dreams to the wind,
he wears them as jewels
on his gentle fingers
and quietly slips them on
the branches he tickles.

Let him adorn our trees
with your emeralds,
in preparation for this season's growth
and the shade required
for the many wanderers seeking respite.

He reaches far,
teasing the forests with your gems,
undressing the blushing orchards
and flirtatious groves,
one day returning
to softly kiss your lips,
the ardent one
that once gave him life.

INVINCIBLE

A Queen awakens
in the city of jewels
where choice
revels in divine will
and power is ample.

For centuries the blue-eyed,
hooded brothers
have guarded her throne room,
but I hear when she arose
from her slumber
they lost their position.

Tear open the chest
of your heart's inheritance,
with blades of revolt.

Take back your life-giving body
with spears of valor.

The victim in your head
should run.

THROB

The brimming village woman
roars her ballads as she grinds,
while the slaves of flamenco
throw down their staccato.

The romantics
pound their ebony and bone
with reverent delirium
and the street saints
thump their buckets.

Get up,
those tapping toes
and that bopping head
quiver at the sound
of your heart's drum.

Sway,
bounce,
and lose yourself
in a song
you thought you never knew.

SURRENDER

Bid
farewell,
lovingly,
to the edge
you grip
so tightly
in this final
attempt to
survive.
The new
will
catch you
in the giant,
restless
hands of
God.

WHEN HORSES RUN

I know
love is foreign
to your strained ears
and many unwanted squatters
have ambushed your gates.
Let me blow my verse
into your sorrow
and sweep a path
for the Beloved,
who wildly rides towards you
on the billowing hair of running horses,
smashing the traitors
who obstruct ascension
to a seat
in your generous court.

VICTORY

Strange,
how this courage
is the bringer of a
beautiful heartache,
the necessary defeat
to win the divine.
That "no,"
a seeming break,
has become
the queen
of my chessboard.
And you, my friend,
are out of moves.

PRANKS AND CRIMES

Unite
with this contented caravan
of religious delinquents
traveling
the invisible bridge
from one heart
to the next,
delivering the news
of our unruly love,
capturing the desperate
with our rumble,
ever extending an offer
to weep together,
as we fearlessly lose
our epic duels with
the divine.

MIDNIGHT BLOSSOM

Dine
with lovers
under this lush
trellis of night blossoms,
sharing the harvest
from today's prayers.
Drink,
a rare vintage of
bliss
is poured
into many cups.
Relish
together,
as you fill that
splendid belly
with earth's
bounty.
Gather.
Call them with your joy.
All are welcome
at this feast,
the table stretches for miles.

A POEM'S MYSTERY

Write
as if you are
your own lover.

This quill's affection for
the paper has made me sane.

I exhilarate the ink with
each stroke
emancipating Venus from my cells.

I catch up to the horizon with
each line
sending my verse soaring over the edge,
to nuzzle the Sun,
so that he will paint his pleasure
across the sky.

Write, I beg you,
Write.

Compose your soul's freedom.

The Beloved burns
for your poems.

CHASED

I escaped,

you pursued.

I ran,

you came looking.

I hid,

you searched and found.

I fell,

you gave me wings.

We fly.

Am I so irresistible,

Beloved,

or are you?

HERE

Trusting
what's to come,
grateful for
what has been
and brings
me here today,
I sit in this instant,
larger than the heavens,
smaller than the atom's moons,
catching bolts
from the thunderous laughter
in God's enormous belly.

SAVAGE COMPASSION

Heart,
you are fierce.
There is the brutal and
ecstatic blow
in defiance of all that dishonors me,
thrusting me into
the sultry void,
chest torn open
so the Beloved may dance
on the altar there,
while I lay
motionless.
Bound.
Gutted.
Utterly aroused.

SEEN

Come Beloved,
make love to me as men seldom can.
Sear my soul with those ravenous eyes,
wet for the sacred I hold.
Entrench the hills of my body
with the tremble in your fingers,
and offend my caverns
with the salt of your ocean.
Spread my throbbing limbs
with the weight of your love,
anoint my flesh
with tears of devotion
and garland me with your sighs.
Exhaust me with the fever of
your immaculate desire.
Enter.
Thunder.
Claim.
Ah,
here I am.

ACKNOWLEDGEMENTS

Thank you Gurumayi Chidvilasananda for teaching me to connect to the heart, for inspiring me to write through your poetry and music, and for encouraging my creativity. This book is possible through your grace, love, and support.

Thank you to Govind Dada and Lakshmi Ma, Dayalji Bapu and Sita Ba, and Daya Dada and Devi Ma for teaching me about courage. I am what I am today because of your vision, sacrifice and fearless steps towards a better future for yourselves and others.

Thank you Mom and Dad for your patience and generosity. Thank you for teaching me about service and how to work from joy. Thank you for giving this book wings.

Thank you Ameet and Swathi for your support. Ameet, I was able to write this collection because of your shelter—figuratively and literally. You single handedly squashed the notion of a "starving artist."

Thank you Holly Payne for your trust. Thank you for giving my art and heart a platform through Skywriter Books. Thank you for guiding this collection to the summit.

Thank you Zack Rogow for your poetic passion and rigor. Thank you for teaching me the art of surprise. Your knowledge and insight throughout the editing process has strengthened the collection as well as my life.

Thank you Angela Zusman for helping me free my voice. I wrote this collection because of your question – "Ushi, what *should* you write and what do you *want* to write?" Thank you Gail Ann for a similar spark – "Ushi, you are doing so many great things, but are you happy doing them?"

Thank you Anjali, Angelina, Carrie, Mona, Monica, Neka, Paula, Paige and Shelly - sisters from another mother, b-f-f-s, and my soul caravan. Thank you Sally and Dr. Timothy Dukes for your navigation through the mountains of Marin and life.

Thank you Katherine and Rodrigo aka "Boo." Thank you for dreaming with me and reminding me why I do what I do. Thank you for the laughter. Thank you for the partnership, friendship and adventure.

Thank you to my talent squad. To the tower of Seans – Curley for your coding genius and Mikula for the gorgeous photos. To Julie Munsayac for a hauntingly-beautiful cover and interior. To Dionisio Ceballos for a moving and magnificent video trailer. To Erica Ekrem at Odelae for your creation of the exquisite, handcrafted, leather-bound collection of *Brave the Unknown*.

Thank you all. This collection is a reflection of your love and belief.

EVIDENCE

The peaceful rhythm
of my feet on the earth
near the river's edge
persuades me of life's reason.

Rumi, I whirl in your field.
And dear Hafiz
I am drunk from your wine.
Exalted Mirabai, I disappear
into your words.
Lady Angelou, I have secured
the diamond between my legs
and Madame Mary,
I have saved the only life I could.
And you,
Queen of Hearts,
sculptor of bliss,
I spark by your lightning.

Ever an apprentice,
I rest on the roots of
the mother eucalyptus,

and dream again.

CPSIA information can be obtained at www.ICGtesting.com
Printed in the USA
BVOW02s0313190813

328794BV00001B/17/P